Debt-Free in a Year

A Comprehensive Financial Freedom Guide

Thomas Sam

TABLE OF CONTENTS

INTRODUCTION

Welcome to "Debt-Free in a Year: A Comprehensive Financial Freedom Guide." In an era where financial burdens can often feel insurmountable, this guide is a beacon of hope and a roadmap towards achieving lasting financial stability.

The weight of debt can be overwhelming, affecting every aspect of our lives from emotional well-being to future aspirations. This guide is meticulously crafted to empower individuals with the knowledge and strategies necessary to break free from the chains of debt within a year.

Navigating the complex landscape of personal finance requires more than just budgeting tips; it demands a holistic approach that encompasses understanding the psychology of spending, implementing effective debt repayment techniques, and cultivating long-term financial habits. This guide goes beyond traditional advice, offering practical insights tailored to various financial situations and personalities.

Authored by financial experts who have themselves triumphed over debt, this guide merges tried-and-true methods with innovative perspectives. From creating realistic debt-reduction plans to rebuilding credit scores and fostering a healthier relationship with money, each chapter is a step towards reclaiming financial independence.

Embark on this transformative journey, and in just a year, you could be well on your way to a debt-free life, laying the foundation for a future of financial success and peace of mind.

CHAPTER ONE

Facing the Debt Dilemma: Understanding Your Financial Landscape

In an age marked by consumerism and easy access to credit, the burden of debt has become an ever-present reality for individuals and families alike. The opening chapter of "Debt-Free in a Year: A Comprehensive Financial Freedom Guide" initiates a profound exploration into the heart of the debt dilemma, recognizing that comprehending your financial landscape is the pivotal first step on your path to debt freedom. This chapter unveils the intricate facets of debt, enabling you to grasp its multifaceted implications, its influence on your financial well-being, and its potential to hinder the realization of your goals and dreams.

The Varied Types of Debts: Navigating a Complex Terrain

Debt is not a monolithic entity; it manifests in various forms, each with its own distinct characteristics and implications. From credit card debt and student loans to mortgages and personal loans, understanding the nuances of these different types of debts is paramount. In this chapter, we shed light on the intricacies of each debt category, elucidating their terms, interest rates, and repayment structures. By demystifying these financial intricacies, we empower you to differentiate between manageable and detrimental forms of debt.

Impact on Financial Health: Unveiling the Hidden Costs

While the immediate impact of debt is evident in the balance sheets and monthly payments, its repercussions can infiltrate numerous aspects of your life. This chapter delves into the hidden costs of debt, beyond the monetary realm. From the emotional toll of constant financial stress to the strain it places on relationships, debt's far-reaching consequences are examined. By comprehending the toll it takes on mental and emotional well-being, you gain a holistic understanding of why seeking freedom from debt is not solely about the numbers on a page.

Debt as an Impediment to Goals: Navigating Dreams Deferred

Debt can act as a formidable barrier between you and your aspirations. It has the potential to postpone your dreams, restrict your life choices, and undermine your long-term goals. By dissecting the ways in which debt can hinder your ability to pursue further education, start a business, buy a home, or even enjoy simple pleasures, this chapter underscores the urgency of breaking free from its grasp. It's not just about achieving financial independence; it's about reclaiming agency over your life choices.

Psychology of Spending and Debt Accumulation: Unmasking Behavioral Patterns

Understanding debt involves delving into the psychology of spending, which often intertwines with the accumulation of debt. This chapter delves deep into the behavioral patterns that lead to excessive spending and, consequently, debt accumulation. From the allure of instant gratification to the societal pressures of keeping up appearances, we help you recognize the triggers and tendencies that might have led you into debt. This self-awareness forms the cornerstone of your journey towards debt freedom.

Breaking the Cycle: A Journey to Empowerment

The first step towards resolving any issue is acknowledging its existence. By exposing the layers of the debt dilemma, this chapter empowers you with the knowledge necessary to confront your financial situation head-on. Armed with a comprehensive understanding of the types of debts, their impacts, and the behavioral patterns that contribute to their accumulation, you're equipped to make informed decisions about your financial future. This chapter isn't merely about highlighting the challenges; it's about laying the foundation for a transformative journey towards lasting financial freedom.

In essence, the opening chapter of "Debt-Free in a Year: A Comprehensive Financial Freedom Guide" serves as a guiding light, illuminating the complex terrain of debt and its profound influence on your life. By unveiling the layers of debt's impact on your financial health, goals, dreams, and behaviors, we invite you to embark on a journey of self-discovery and empowerment. Armed with this understanding, you're prepared to take the subsequent steps towards crafting a strategic plan for debt reduction, rebuilding your financial foundation, and ultimately achieving the coveted state of debt freedom.

CHAPTER TWO

Crafting Your Roadmap to Debt Freedom: Building a Solid Financial Plan

With the foundation laid in understanding your financial landscape and the intricacies of debt, it's time to embark on a transformative journey towards reclaiming control over your financial future. The second chapter of "Debt-Free in a Year: A Comprehensive Financial Freedom Guide" introduces you to the essential process of crafting a roadmap to debt freedom. In this chapter, we navigate the intricacies of creating a comprehensive financial plan, meticulously tailored to your unique circumstances. From setting realistic debt reduction goals to analyzing your income, expenses, and existing debts, we equip you with the tools to construct a strategic plan that will propel you towards your debt-free aspirations.

The Power of Setting Realistic Debt Reduction Goals

The journey to debt freedom begins with setting clear and achievable goals. In this section, we delve into the importance of establishing realistic debt reduction targets. By setting goals that align with your financial capacity and life circumstances, you create a roadmap that not only motivates you but also prevents discouragement and burnout. Whether your goals involve paying off specific debts, reducing your debt-to-income ratio, or achieving a certain credit score, the process of goal setting empowers you to measure your progress and celebrate milestones along the way.

Analyzing Your Financial Landscape: Income, Expenses, and Debts

A comprehensive financial plan hinges on a thorough analysis of your current financial standing. This section guides you through the process of evaluating your income streams and expenses. By scrutinizing your income sources, you gain insights into your earning potential and identify avenues for potential growth. Simultaneously, assessing your expenses allows you to pinpoint areas where cuts can be made, freeing up resources for debt repayment.

Central to this analysis is an in-depth examination of your existing debts. We guide you through creating a detailed inventory of your debts, including outstanding balances, interest rates, and minimum monthly payments. This comprehensive overview of your financial obligations forms the bedrock upon which your debt reduction strategy will be built.

Tailoring the Plan to Your Unique Circumstances

A one-size-fits-all approach to debt reduction is rarely effective. Every individual's financial situation is distinct, necessitating a personalized plan. This section underscores the importance of tailoring your financial plan to your unique circumstances. Whether you're a recent graduate with student loans, a homeowner with a mortgage, or someone grappling with credit card debt, your plan must address your specific challenges and opportunities.

We explore various debt repayment strategies that cater to diverse situations. For instance, the snowball method, which involves prioritizing the repayment of smaller debts first to build momentum, might be ideal for some. Others might benefit more from the avalanche method, where debts with the highest interest rates are tackled first to minimize long-term costs. By understanding these strategies, you're empowered to choose the one that aligns with your financial objectives and psychological motivations.

Prioritizing and Consolidating Debts: A Strategic Approach

Dealing with multiple debts can feel overwhelming, and that's where prioritization and consolidation come into play. This section introduces the concept of prioritizing debts based on factors like interest rates, outstanding balances, and potential impact on credit score. By strategically allocating your resources towards high-priority debts, you optimize your progress towards debt freedom.

Additionally, the chapter explores the concept of debt consolidation – combining multiple debts into a single, more manageable payment. This can simplify your financial landscape, reduce the risk of missed payments, and potentially lower interest rates. However, it's crucial to understand the nuances of consolidation before embarking on this path.

Steady Progress Towards Debt Freedom: Your Personalized Roadmap

As you work through this chapter, you gradually build your personalized roadmap to debt freedom. Armed with insights into goal setting, a comprehensive analysis of your financial situation, and a strategic plan for debt reduction, you're prepared to take the subsequent steps in your journey. This roadmap serves not only as a guide for the months ahead but also as a source of motivation, reminding you that each step you take brings you closer to the ultimate goal of being debt-free.

In essence, the second chapter of "Debt-Free in a Year: A Comprehensive Financial Freedom Guide" equips you with the foundational tools to construct a financial plan that is both realistic and adaptable. By setting clear goals, analyzing your financial landscape, tailoring your plan to your circumstances, and strategically addressing your debts, you're well-prepared to navigate the challenges and triumphs that lie ahead. This chapter isn't just about creating a plan; it's about laying the groundwork for a transformative journey towards lasting financial freedom.

CHAPTER THREE

Strategies for Swift Debt Repayment: Techniques That Work

In the pursuit of financial freedom, the path to debt repayment is a critical phase that demands strategic thinking, dedication, and disciplined execution. Chapter 3 of "Debt-Free in a Year: A Comprehensive Financial Freedom Guide" serves as a beacon of practical guidance, delving deep into actionable strategies that have been proven to expedite the debt repayment journey. Whether you're contending with credit card debt, student loans, or any other financial obligations, this chapter provides you with a comprehensive overview of techniques that can significantly accelerate your progress towards a debt-free life.

The Snowball Method: Momentum through Small Wins

At the heart of this chapter lies the snowball method, a strategy that centers on the psychological power of small wins. The concept is simple yet effective: start by paying off your smallest debt while continuing to make minimum payments on your other debts. As the smaller debt is eliminated, you redirect the funds towards the next smallest debt, creating a snowball effect that gains momentum with each victory.

The snowball method goes beyond pure financial calculations; it taps into human psychology. By experiencing quick wins, you build confidence, motivation, and a sense of accomplishment that fuels your commitment to debt repayment. This method can be particularly beneficial if you find yourself demotivated by larger debts with lengthier repayment timelines.

The Avalanche Method: Minimizing Long-Term Costs

While the snowball method emphasizes psychology, the avalanche method is driven by cold, hard mathematics. With this approach, you prioritize debts based on their interest rates. Begin by focusing on the debt with the highest interest rate, as it incurs the most significant long-term costs. By attacking high-interest debts first, you minimize the overall interest you'll pay over time.

The avalanche method is particularly suited for those who are comfortable taking a more calculated approach, valuing long-term savings over immediate emotional victories. While it might take longer to see tangible results compared to the snowball method, the avalanche method ensures that you optimize your financial resources for the most efficient debt reduction.

The Hybrid Approach: Combining Strategies for Maximum Impact

Recognizing that personal finance is rarely one-size-fits-all, this chapter introduces the hybrid approach—a harmonious integration of the snowball and avalanche methods. With this strategy, you benefit from the psychological rewards of the snowball method while also capitalizing on the financial efficiency of the avalanche method.

In the hybrid approach, you begin by addressing your smallest debt, gaining an early sense of accomplishment. Afterward, you transition to the avalanche method, prioritizing debts based on their interest rates. This balanced approach strikes a chord between motivation and optimization, providing the best of both worlds for individuals seeking a comprehensive solution.

Budgeting: The Foundation of Swift Debt Repayment

While debt repayment strategies are essential, their effectiveness hinges on a solid foundation:

budgeting. This chapter underscores the significance of creating a comprehensive budget that reflects your income, expenses, and debt obligations. By meticulously tracking where your money goes, you gain control over your financial inflows and outflows, enabling you to allocate resources strategically.

Budgeting serves as a roadmap that guides your spending decisions, prevents overspending, and identifies areas where you can trim unnecessary expenses. With a well-structured budget, you're better equipped to channel more resources towards debt elimination, intensifying the impact of your chosen debt repayment strategy.

Expense Tracking: Illuminating Spending Patterns

In conjunction with budgeting, expense tracking sheds light on your spending patterns. This practice involves meticulously recording every expense, no matter how small, to gain a holistic understanding of where your money is being allocated. This chapter delves into the tools and methods available for effective expense tracking, whether it's through apps, spreadsheets, or dedicated financial software.

By tracking expenses, you uncover patterns that might have previously gone unnoticed. This awareness empowers you to identify potential areas for cost-cutting, directing more funds towards debt repayment. Expense tracking, when combined with budgeting, forms a powerful duo that not only accelerates debt repayment but also nurtures financial mindfulness.

Informed Spending Choices: Cultivating Financial Discipline

A pivotal aspect of swift debt repayment involves making informed spending choices. This chapter emphasizes the significance of being intentional with your expenditures and distinguishing between needs and wants. By practicing mindful spending, you curtail impulsive purchases and free up resources that can be channeled towards your debt elimination goals.

Making conscious choices about how you allocate your money is an exercise in financial discipline. It reinforces your commitment to becoming debt-free and empowers you to view each purchase as a step either towards or away from that goal. Through a combination of budgeting, expense tracking, and mindful spending, you maximize the impact of your debt repayment strategy.

Embracing Techniques for Swift Debt Repayment

"Debt-Free in a Year: A Comprehensive Financial Freedom Guide" goes beyond theory, delving into actionable techniques that facilitate your journey to debt freedom. By exploring the snowball method, avalanche method, and the hybrid approach, you're presented with a versatile toolkit to suit your preferences and motivations. Moreover, the chapter emphasizes the foundational role of budgeting, expense tracking, and informed spending choices in intensifying the impact of your chosen strategy.

As you navigate the complexities of debt repayment, these techniques serve as pillars of support, guiding you towards a debt-free life with strategic precision and newfound financial empowerment. By embracing these strategies, you not only expedite your journey but also cultivate a lasting understanding of how financial mindfulness and discipline can shape a more secure and prosperous future.

CHAPTER FOUR

Rebuilding Your Financial Foundation: Nurturing Credit and Savings

While the pursuit of debt freedom remains a cornerstone of financial empowerment, the journey is multifaceted. In Chapter 4 of "Debt-Free in a Year: A Comprehensive Financial Freedom Guide," the spotlight turns towards rebuilding your financial foundation. This critical phase involves nurturing your credit score, constructing a safety net through emergency funds, and cultivating a robust habit of saving. As you progress towards debt freedom, these actions not only prevent future debt traps but also lay the groundwork for long-term financial security and success.

Rebuilding Your Credit Score: Unlocking Financial Opportunities

Your credit score is more than just a three-digit number; it's a gateway to financial opportunities. Chapter 4 takes a magnifying glass to the intricate realm of credit scores, unveiling the mechanisms that determine your score and its far-reaching implications. Rebuilding your credit score is a strategic endeavor that paves the way for securing favorable interest rates, accessing loans, and even impacting your housing and job prospects.

This chapter delves into practical strategies for improving your credit score. From reviewing your credit report for inaccuracies to establishing a history of responsible credit usage, you'll gain insights into steps that can propel your score upwards. Understanding the factors that influence your credit score empowers you to take targeted actions that not only contribute to debt freedom but also set the stage for your future financial endeavors.

Emergency Fund: Building a Safety Net

In the pursuit of financial freedom, unexpected setbacks can be a formidable challenge. This is where the concept of an emergency fund comes into play. Chapter 4 places a spotlight on the significance of building a robust emergency fund—a financial cushion that safeguards you against unforeseen events such as medical emergencies, job loss, or major repairs.

Creating an emergency fund is not merely an option; it's a foundational step towards financial resilience. This chapter guides you through determining the ideal size of your emergency fund, taking into consideration factors like monthly expenses, potential risks, and individual circumstances. By setting aside funds for unexpected situations, you not only mitigate the risk of falling back into debt but also cultivate a sense of confidence and stability in the face of uncertainty.

Cultivating a Habit of Saving: Paving the Way for Prosperity

The practice of saving transcends the realm of emergency funds—it's a daily habit that shapes your financial trajectory. Chapter 4 underscores the value of cultivating a consistent habit of saving. Whether it's for short-term goals like vacations or long-term aspirations like homeownership, saving forms the bedrock of financial prosperity.

This chapter offers practical insights into jumpstarting your savings journey. It delves into the art of setting achievable saving goals, automating your savings contributions, and exploring different savings vehicles such as high-yield savings accounts or retirement funds. By making saving a non-negotiable part of your financial routine, you gradually accumulate the resources needed not only to achieve your dreams but also to weather unexpected storms without derailing your progress.

Future-Proofing Your Financial Well-Being

As you traverse the path to debt freedom, Chapter 4 serves as a guidepost to ensure that your journey isn't merely a short-term accomplishment but a lasting transformation. By rebuilding your credit score, constructing an emergency fund, and nurturing a savings habit, you fortify your financial foundation against potential setbacks and unforeseen challenges.

This chapter transcends immediate goals, reminding you that the pursuit of debt freedom is interwoven with the quest for lasting financial security and well-being. By understanding the intricate dynamics of credit scores, embracing the concept of an emergency fund, and fostering a culture of saving, you're better equipped to navigate the complexities of financial life beyond debt. These actions empower you to seize opportunities, navigate unexpected turns, and ultimately forge a future marked by resilience, prosperity, and the freedom to pursue your aspirations with unwavering confidence.

CHAPTER FIVE

Sustaining Financial Wellness: Habits for a Debt-Free Future

As you approach the culmination of your journey to debt freedom, the final chapter of "Debt-Free in a Year: A Comprehensive Financial Freedom Guide" becomes an indispensable compass for navigating the future. Chapter 5 is more than a conclusion—it's a pivotal guide dedicated to ensuring that your triumph over debt is not a fleeting accomplishment but a lasting transformation. In this chapter, we delve into the habits and mindsets essential for maintaining your newfound financial wellness. By exploring effective money management practices and fostering a positive relationship with money, you're equipped to not only steer clear of returning to debt but also to advance towards a future marked by enduring financial freedom.

Cultivating Effective Money Management Practices

Central to sustaining financial wellness is the cultivation of effective money management practices. This section offers insights into creating and maintaining a budget that aligns with your post-debt financial landscape. By continuing to track your income, expenses, and debt repayments, you remain in control of your finances and ensure that you're living within your means.

Beyond budgeting, this chapter underscores the importance of mindful spending. We delve into strategies for making conscious purchasing decisions, differentiating between needs and wants, and adopting a more deliberate approach to consumerism. These practices not only prevent overspending but also free up resources that can be channeled towards saving and investing, further enhancing your financial stability.

Building and Sustaining Emergency Funds

While you may have established an emergency fund during your journey to debt freedom, maintaining and replenishing this fund is equally vital in the post-debt era. This section explores strategies for consistently contributing to your emergency fund and ensuring it remains a reliable safety net. We delve into the dynamics of balancing short-term goals with the long-term security that an adequately funded emergency fund provides.

Recognizing that emergencies and unexpected expenses are an inevitable part of life, this chapter empowers you to remain vigilant and proactive in safeguarding your financial well-being. By sustaining your emergency fund, you reduce the risk of being forced back into debt due to unforeseen circumstances.

Nurturing a Positive Relationship with Money

Your journey to debt freedom is not solely about numerical achievements; it's also about transforming your relationship with money. This section delves into the mindset shifts necessary to foster a healthier connection with your financial resources. By embracing a positive view of money, reframing your beliefs about wealth, and appreciating the value of financial education, you pave the way for enduring financial well-being.

We also explore strategies for practicing gratitude for your financial progress and avoiding the pitfalls of comparison and materialism. By cultivating contentment and focusing on your unique financial journey, you're less likely to succumb to the pressures of consumer culture and make impulsive decisions that could lead to future debt.

Continued Education and Growth

As you transition from debt burden to financial freedom, the quest for knowledge remains paramount. This section emphasizes the significance of continued financial education and growth. By staying informed about personal finance trends, investment opportunities, and strategies for wealth accumulation, you empower yourself to make informed decisions that align with your long-term goals.

Additionally, this chapter touches on the importance of adapting your financial strategies as your circumstances evolve. Life is dynamic, and your financial plan should reflect this reality. Regularly revisiting and adjusting your budget, savings goals, and investment strategies ensures that your financial foundation remains strong, even in the face of changing situations.

Securing Your Debt-Free Future

This Chapter not only celebrates your journey to debt freedom but also sets the stage for the chapters yet to be written in your financial story. By embracing effective money management practices, nurturing a positive relationship with money, and committing to ongoing education and growth, you not only prevent the recurrence of debt but also advance towards lasting financial wellness.

A debt-free journey is a lifelong pursuit—one that continues to unfold with each intentional decision you make. By incorporating these habits and mindsets into your daily life, you create a sustainable framework for a future defined by financial empowerment, security, and the freedom to pursue your dreams without the weight of debt.